SOME MEN NEED HELP

by

John Ford Noonan

SAMUEL FRENCH, INC.
45 West 25th Street NEW YORK 10010
7623 Sunset Boulevard HOLLYWOOD 90046
LONDON TORONTO

ISBN 0 573 64037 8

Printed in U.S.A.

47th Street Theatre

304 West 47th Street

Frank Gero Mark Gero Chris Gero
in association with Jane Holzer
present

PHILIP BOSCO & TREAT WILLIAMS

in

SOME MEN NEED HELP

by

John Ford Noonan

Set Design by Eugene Lee
Lighting Design by Gregory C. MacPhearson
Costume Design by Shay Cunliffe
Original Music by Richard Weinstock
Fights Staged by B. H. Barry
Directed by John Ferraro

CAST

(IN ORDER OF APPEARANCE)

Hudley T. Singleton III . . . . TREAT WILLIAMS
Gaetano Altobelli . . . . PHILIP BOSCO

CHARACTERS

(in order of their appearance)

Hudley T. Singleton, III

Gaetano Altobelli

TIME

ACT I

LATE SEPTEMBER

Scene 1: Monday morning, just after 9 A.M.

Scene 2: Tuesday, 9 A.M.

Scene 3: Wednesday, 10:30 A.M.

ACT II

ALMOST THREE MONTHS LATER, THE WEEK BETWEEN CHRISTMAS AND NEW YEAR'S

Scene 1: Thursday, 2 P.M.

Scene 2: Friday, just before 9A.M.

Scene 3: A few days later, just after the first of the year, early afternoon

PLACE

77 Huckleberry Drive, Roman Hills,
Fairfield County, Conneticut

SOME MEN NEED HELP

by

John Ford Noonan

ACT I

Scene 1

The place is a two-story home in suburbia. The address is 77 Huckleberry Drive in the fictional town of Roman Hills in a busy area of Connecticut known as Fairfield County. Late September. Monday, 9 A.M.

Lights up! HUDLEY T. SINGLETON, III's kitchen, the kind found in BETTER HOMES AND GARDENS. The kitchen is a true catastrophe. A month of daily N.Y. TIMES thrown against broom closet. Broken vodka bottles under table. Dishes stacked in sink. Counter overflows with beer cans and about 21 empty boxes from Chinese dinners. Screen on door with hole punched in it. HUDLEY asleep on floor, passed out from a night of heavy drinking. Clothes disheveled, he twitches, stabs hands out, talks non-sequiturs. Several seconds and GAETANO ALTOBELLI appears at kitchen door, dressed in suit, tie and wearing expensive jewelry. GAETANO carries a small red package. He knocks loudly. HUDLEY gets to his feet and crosses to door...

GAETANO. Hi, Hud!

HUDLEY. How do you know my name?

GAETANO. How's it going?

HUDLEY. Is there something you want?

GAETANO. Brought you a present.

HUDLEY. Have we ever met?

GAETANO. You'll open it up. You'll say to yourself, "Hud, how the heck could he have known?" That's me: Knowing the last thing about you that you expect me to know. I remember one time. I was in Ohio on business. Steubenville. A case of late payments. Knew the guy I was after had a wife addicted to licorice. Now when I knock on his door, I got a big, long piece sticking out. He opens. I say, "Guess what I know!" Guy pays up without a word. Brings to mind another time. Miami Beach. Heighth of the season. Case of disappearing minks. Franky Topcoat was upset so me and Danny W., we take off on Eastern. Plane lands. Light as a feather. We taxi over to the departure dock. There's a delay. Me and Danny W., we sit back and reflect on stewardesses the world over. Eastern stewardesses are the best, hands down. Curviest figures, nicest smiles. We decide to make a move on the two up by the door. The one I pick I grab by the wrist and whisper, "You like it but you don't make a lotta noise!" She has me on the floor before the captain can alert traffic control. Knowing the last thing about people they expect you to know, it's a big edge.

HUDLEY. Excuse me but --

GAETANO. Go on, give her a feel.

HUDLEY. Beg pardon?

GAETANO. Guess what's for you? *(holding up present-*

wrapped package to screen door) When I was a kid, my nickname was "Hands". What a pair. Friends were always bringing things by for me to feel up -- "Hands, tell us what we're in for." Those were the days. Had a Schwinn for a bike: Twenty-six inch wheels, crash bars, streamers from the grips. Listen, give her a feel and then we can -- *(He reaches for handle on screen door.)*

(HUDLEY intercepts action by holding door tight from the inside.)

GAETANO. You're holding the door.

HUDLEY. I'm not. My hand is.

GAETANO. Hudley, tell your hand to let go.

HUDLEY. Exactly who are you?

GAETANO. Find out. Ask me in.

HUDLEY. That's what I love about you Italians!

GAETANO. Who says I'm Italian?

HUDLEY. You can pick up the garbage and cut my lawn but absolutely none of you is allowed in my kitchen. Don't drip olive oil on the flagstone walk as you're leaving. *(He locks latch on screen door, crosses back to kitchen table, sweeps salt and pepper, flower piece, etc. onto floor with a loud crash. Head down, loud snoring, he is instantly asleep.)*

(GAETANO kicks open door, tearing latch from door. He enters. In one hand, small surprise package wrapped in red paper.)

HUDLEY. You'll pay to have that fixed.

GAETANO. The check's already in the mail. *(He rushes over to sink, screams out, lifts smelly, greasy frying pan from sink.)*

When did you use this, the last time Columbus visited New York? A guy with your education, background, living like this; what would your mother think?

HUDLEY. She's dead.

GAETANO. According to you! For all we know she's trapped behind here somewhere. *(He suddenly pulls plastic bag from inside jacket and begins sweeping Chinese food containers, bottles and cans from counter top into bag.)*

HUDLEY. Buster, you can't come in someone's private home and start --

GAETANO. First off, let me shake your hand. *(grabbing HUDLEY'S hand)* Greatest white dancer in the free world. The wiggles. The stomps. The leaps. The splits. I was watching the whole bar watch you. There wasn't a pair of eyes you didn't make happy. Even my limo driver, Danny Wheels, cheered. Remember how he kept begging you to do it all over again? Everyone else was up for it too. Four more quarters in the juke and you were even greater the second time. Higher leaps. Bigger wiggles. My only question is why?

HUDLEY. Why what?

GAETANO. Why dance so great and not want to remember it?

HUDLEY. Of course I --

GAETANO. Remember trying to jump out of my limo coming down Reef Road, yes or no?!

HUDLEY. Are you suggesting that you brought me home last night?

GAETANO. How many times did *she* have to bring you home? My people tell me it got to be two or three times a week towards the end.

HUDLEY. Towards the end of what?

GAETANO. Kate's left you three times in the past two years. Was the reason always the same?

HUDLEY. Mister, what I do with my nights is none --

GAETANO. What's the last sentence you spoke last night you can be sure of?

HUDLEY. As I recall --

GAETANO. We put you to bed! How did you end up here on the floor? Have you smelled your hands?

(HUDLEY smells hands.)

GAETANO. Who held you in the shower? How many times did you vomit? How much of it did you eat?

(HUDLEY bursts out of room.)

GAETANO. *(Runs to door and yells up stairs.)* Hit the bowl this time! *(He returns to cleaning countertops of old garbage, singing his favorite Italian song.)*

HUDLEY. *(Brief seconds and he races back, drying face with towel. Begins to laugh.)* Yuck, yuck, yuck. It's a joke on me. Ha, ha, ha.

GAETANO. Like the way we stretched on the clean sheets, real tight in all the corners?

HUDLEY. And my clothes all hung in my closet just the way I do it? However, who wrote that disgusting note on the mirror?

GAETANO. What note?

HUDLEY. See, anyone can play your game. *(He laughs.)*

(GAETANO laughs back, the two men getting louder and louder.)

HUDLEY. Mister, who sent you? I want a name.

GAETANO. All that matters is that I'm here in time.

HUDLEY. Get out of my house. NOW! *(He starts toward GAETANO.)*

(GAETANO suddenly goes to his pocket as if he were reaching for a gun.)

HUDLEY. Italians! When you can't handle what you're feeling, you pull a gun. You going to pull a gun?

(GAETANO laughs.)

HUDLEY. I'll pay you to shoot me. Go on, everything I have in my pocket. *(He reaches into pocket, bringing out money clip and change, counting quickly.)* How's $72.20 for a hit, gangland-style? Blood on the table, blood on the floor, a smirk on the dead WASP's face?!

(GAETANO quickly withdraws hand from breast pocket. Hand contains bright red handkerchief. HUDLEY gasps, jumps back.)

GAETANO. *(Laughs, tosses handkerchief to HUDLEY.)* Wipe your forehead. Sweat's not you.

(HUDLEY races to cabinet over counter. Opens door, reaches in expecting to find hidden pint of vodka; finds nothing. Throws

entire contents of cabinet on floor. HUDLEY now ravages other cabinets, hurling contents to floor, finding nothing. All his secret stashes of vodka have been removed.)

GAETANO. How's it feel?

HUDLEY. You can't just --- just --- This is AMERICA!

GAETANO. No, it's not. It's Fairfield County.

HUDLEY. *(starting toward phone on wall)* I'm calling the police.

GAETANO. Ask for Sergeant Jim Borelli. He's the one who arrested you August 14 for hitting your wife.

HUDLEY. It wasn't as simple as that!

GAETANO. Tell him you're also the same guy he arrested at Fairfield Yacht Club July 4th for indecent exposure.

HUDLEY. O.K., O.K.! *Once* I went a little too far.

GAETANO. *(Takes out paper and reads from it.)* August 26th you kicked Rachel Dean at the A&P and then stuffed her in her shopping cart. September 11, a little over two weeks ago, at Palumbo's Gas Station, you tried, with the hose, to --

HUDLEY. It's been hard without my wife. Without Kate I --

(GAETANO laughs.)

HUDLEY. Why are you laughing?

GAETANO. Months from now, you're going to look back on today and laugh a whole different laugh.

HUDLEY. Why would I laugh?

GAETANO. That's the key: the not forgetting.

HUDLEY. Forgetting what?

GAETANO. I got a feeling you and I are going to end up good friends.

HUDLEY. What are you talking about?!

GAETANO. Tell you one thing: you've driven me and my son close together for the first time.

HUDLEY. What's your son got to do with anything?!!

GAETANO. Carmella, I've pretty much given up on.

HUDLEY. Who's Carmella?

GAETANO. The wife. Yes sir, you've got him to thank.

HUDLEY. Him who?

GAETANO. My son!

HUDLEY. But you just --

GAETANO. Like a drink?

HUDLEY. Actually I --

GAETANO. You look thirsty!!

HUDLEY. *(giving GAETANO the finger)* Nice try.

GAETANO. Other day me and the wife get home from Mulberry Street. She loves me to go back and remember. Anyway, in the living room there's set up all these empty grocery boxes. Tops of tables, chairs, you know, two on the couch. Son says, "You two, sit!" He goes out, charges back in stumbling drunk. Head tilt, wobbly knees, boxes flying. He even does the people screaming. Immediately I laugh. He's doing you at the A&P. I scream, "You're doing Hudley T. from the A&P." He rushes over and hugs me for the first time since I called him "Fatso". Big weight problem. Anyway, I'm touched, crying. He whispers in my ear, "The guy needs help. Give him a look. He's the first thing that's got me worried since the Yanks got rid of Reggie." Not another word. Just waddles off. So, do you?

HUDLEY. You suck, Buddy. You eat it. You eat suck. Dago-faggot-who-can't-even-get-it-up, do you really expect me to believe some teenage kid --

GAETANO. Says he'll lose a pound a day if I can do my magic act on you. *(He exits out kitchen door. Clearly seen through screen, he whistles down driveway. Next, he follows with several hand signals.)*

HUDLEY. What are you doing?

GAETANO. Whatever you need, he'll take care of it.

HUDLEY. *(exiting out door)* Who?

GAETANO. *(returning to kitchen)* Danny Wheels. My driver.

HUDLEY. *(yelling down driveway)* Hey, Dago-faggot-greaseball-wop, move along or I'll --

(HUDLEY returns to kitchen ... as GAETANO removes small, red package from pocket and removes red wrapping paper. It contains a small cassette player and a cassette tape. GAETANO hands HUDLEY the cassette player.)

GAETANO. The best cassette money can buy. *(Next, hands him cassette tape.)* Here's a tape of a few things you may have forgotten after you got home last night. Give a real careful ear to the screaming and the stuff about Kate. Hudley, I want you to stay in tonight. Relax. Have a nice meal. I'm sending over a Veal Piccata, salad, garlic bread, the works. Next flip on TV. WOR at 9 has "Lost Weekend". Ray Milland's not you but he was getting paid.

(HUDLEY hurls cassette tape to floor and laughs at GAETANO.

GAETANO bends to pick up cassette tape. Hudley crushes with foot.)

GAETANO. Danny Wheels has another copy out in the limo. Yell if you change your mind.

(HUDLEY next throws cassette player to floor and kicks it across the room.)

GAETANO. Some Japanese might take that personally.

HUDLEY. I specialize in upsetting the less fortunate: Polacks, Guineas, Japs, Jews, I've never memorized the whole list. How's it feel?

GAETANO. How's what feel?

HUDLEY. Thinking you're getting through to me. Pal, I can pretend to be amused by your stink, I can act like I'm listening to all you've got to say, but you and I are on entirely different levels. We can joke, laugh. even play golf together on occasions, but never can we pretend we're equals. I know you people wish we were, but face it: Brooks Brothers will never carry an Italian line.

GAETANO. Same time. See you tomorrow. *(He exits out door.)*

HUDLEY. *(Screams out door after him.)* Crawl back to your salami! You're in over your head!!

(HUDLEY is now alone. About to sit at table, he is suddenly struck by an idea. He leaps up, opens the door to the cabinet under the sink, begins taking out bottles of cleaning fluid and smelling contents in search of hidden vodka. He checks bottle of West Pine, jug of Clorox, Ajax Liquid -- bottle of Lysol

Deodorizing Cleaner. Lysol is the one he's looking for. Returning to table, HUDLEY puts Lysol down and has secret conversation with vodka inside Lysol.)

HUDLEY. Vodka? *(He pretends he's the voice of the vodka.)* "I'M LISTENING." *(as himself)* I'm sorry I left you in there so long. *(Again, as the voice of vodka.)* "YOU BIG, DUMB LUG, JUST GRAB ME AND KISS ME!" *(He takes a huge swig out of Lysol bottle. Again, the voice of the vodka.)* "AGAIN." *(He takes second big gulp of vodka. Again, the voice of vodka.)* "ONE MORE BIG WET ONE!" *(He takes third large swig, speaking as himself.)* God, vodka, do we have fun! *(Again, the voice of vodka.)* "DUMMY, WHAT ABOUT OUR SONG?" *(as himself)* Which one? *(Again, the voice of the vodka.)* "ONE MORE KISS AND I'LL WHISPER IN YOUR EAR." *(He takes another huge swig, then places Lysol to ear as though he were listening to it talk. He reacts to what he has been told and begins singing slow and personal version of Gershwin's "Someone To Watch Over Me".★)*

BLACKOUT

★ *Note: This song is fully protected by copyright. Permission to use it is not included with permission to produce "Some Men Need Help". For rights to use this song, contact Chappell & Co., Inc. 810 Seventh Ave., New York, N.Y. 10019.*

ACT I
Scene 2

Again HUDLEY T. SINGLETON, III'S kitchen. It is Tuesday, 9 A.M., the following day.

Lights up! No one in kitchen. Radio playing quietly. As if on purpose, kitchen has been returned to yesterday's mess. Suddenly from garage, just outside, a car horn blares out. The horn stops. The phone rings. HUDLEY stumbles into kitchen, gasping for air. He reaches phone just as it stops ringing...

HUDLEY. *(into receiver)* Hello? --- Hello? *(Hangs up, dials new number, talks into receiver.)* Did Chucky just call me? --- Tell him if he gets over fast and starts the lawn, for lunch I'll make him one of my special melted ham and cheese. After that -- *(suddenly startled, and a hack of coughing)* Do you realize what you're doing? --- He's saying that out of jealousy cause I'm more of a father to the boy than he could ever be. Mrs. Churchill, your son needs me. I may be the only --- You can't forbid him to cut my lawn. That's it. You'll all be dead by 6 P.M. Even the dog. Him I'll pour gas on first. Now please have Chucky here -- *(suddenly screaming into receiver)* Mrs. Churchill, I hope you get stomach cancer and that you smell so bad at the end, even dogs won't go near you. *(Slams down phone. Has a second attack of coughing.)*

(GAETANO enters quietly and stands at kitchen door. He wears a blue and white Yankee windbreaker and a blue and white Yankee cap. He caries second jacket and second cap. Phone rings again.)

HUDLEY. *(into phone)* Now listen, I know you have --- Mrs. Mingus, I'm cutting my vacation short. Call a company meeting for 10:30 tomorrow. Especially I want Elderbee there. And with a tie on! *(suddenly quiet and serious)* Has she? ... What do you mean "has she what"? Has my wife called? Yes, yes, but you're the one she always checks in with. Now take this down. If she wants me to take her back into this house, the conditions are as follows: *number one*, -- ... Mrs. Mingus, don't. You're You're my secretary. You can't hang up on me! ... Hello? ... Hello?!! *(Slams down phone, turns, sees GAETANO, suddenly has another fit of coughing.)* I just woke up in my garage with the engine running. I could've been dead. I thought you were keeping an eye on me. *(He has another fit of coughing. Goes to cabinet over counter, takes out hidden bottle of vodka, swigs to stop coughing.)* Today I'm turning over a whole new leaf. *(Hides bottle back in cabinet.)* First off, I apologize for last night.

GAETANO. What about Danny Wheels' mother?

HUDLEY. Was she the one in the wheelchair?

GAETANO. Say a prayer her brother Dom the Dentist never hears.

HUDLEY. That wasn't me. That was my dark side. That's

what happens when I drink and forget to eat all day. I let my dark side out of the jar. When you visit her later, I want you to tell her that.

GAETANO. That your dark side got out of the jar?

HUDLEY. When I see her across the restaurant, my good side says, "leave the poor lady alone!" My dark side laughs and says, "do it, do it". Next thing I'm pouring the bowl of spaghetti over her head. She screams. I throw salad down her throat. I stuff garlic bread down her sore old cleavage. I grab the back of the wheelchair. I aim it toward the wall. "Ready, everyone listen for the Wop!" The wheelchair crashes. What a Wop!! That's when someone grabs me. Thank God that's as far as I went!

GAETANO. What about the bottle?

HUDLEY. What bottle?

GAETANO. You threw a bottle of wine that almost hit my wife in the head. Next you started on my son. You called him a Blimp. You told him I was ill-equipped. He cries out, "We're trying to help you. Why are you doing this?" My wife's had it. She goes at you with a fork. That's when you whipped it out!

HUDLEY. Bull!

GAETANO. *(Pulls out polaroid picture from pocket.)* That look like *yours*?!!

(HUDLEY grabs photo. GAETANO takes out cassette player, presses Play button, puts on kitchen table. Loud yelling of people in restaurant, followed by sudden quiet and HUDLEY yelling.)

HUDLEY. *(voice on tape)* I WANT TO DIE. SOMEONE,

PLEASE HELP ME! *(HUDLEY now weeping)* I WANT TO DIE. SOMEONE, PLEASE HELP ME. *(a cry of great pain)* I WANT TO DIE. SOMEONE, PLEASE HELP ME. *(HUDLEY presses Stop button, about to smash cassette, but instead sits at table and hugs cassette like a baby.)*

(A car horn is heard from outside.)

GAETANO. My son's waiting in the limo. He wants to take you to see the Yankees play. *(Sits at table, puts hand on HUDLEY.)* Danny Wheels drives like the wind. Forty-five minutes from now, rounding a curve, my boy'll scream, "LOOK, GUYS, THE STADIUM!" We park, we jump out, we go through the gates. My boy goes to pieces, "GO, YANKS, GO!" We each put an arm around him. Lead him to my box behind the Yankee Dugout. It's infield practice for the Baltimore O's. I go get popcorn and half-a-dozen dogs. My son takes your hand and says "Today's another day. Forget about last night." I get back just as the game starts. It goes by like a blur. Yanks win 5-to-2. Next we're outside Gate 12. A door opens. The Diamond Club. I flash my life-time pass. Several players come over. I know them. They know me. They'll like you. Mean people always gravitate toward each other. There'll be this incredible laughing from the right fielder. Right fielders always have these incredible laughs. All of a sudden a hand will hit your shoulder. *(He jumps up, puts hand on HUDLEY'S shoulder.)* Before you can look up, you'll hear, "Hi, Hudley. Glad you could make it."

HUDLEY. Whose hand is it?

GAETANO. The Yanks big RBI man. He'll take you into a

private room. Used to have the same problem himself. Cost him the three best years of his career.

HUDLEY. I was quite a ballplayer myself. I starred at Brown. Twice I was All-East. My senior year I was very closely scouted by both Oakland and --

GAETANO. He'll go over why you can't do it alone.

HUDLEY. Do what alone?

(Again car horn is heard outside.)

GAETANO. *(Puts Yankee jacket over HUDLEY'S shoulders.)* Put this on. Make you feel more part of things.

HUDLEY. *(throwing jacket to ground)* Why do you keep talking to me like I'm one of them? I definitely am not one of them. All that begging and admitting. The door always closed. I'm just --- just going through a rough period. Some days I get a little lost. Once in a while my dark side pushes me out of the way. But -- but I'm on my way back. Starting tomorrow it's only beer and a little light wine. When Kate hears I'm cutting back to only beer and a little light -- *(suddenly laughs)* O God, I should've guessed!

GAETANO. Guessed *WHAT*?

HUDLEY. It's her!

GAETANO. Her *WHO*?

HUDLEY. She put you up to this. Hired you. Paid money. Talked you into it. Wellesley girls can open any door. Yes sir, my little Katie got you to come by. Act tough. Try and scare me into slowing down.

GAETANO. I'm here cause of my son. We live down the road. Third house on the left just before --

HUDLEY. What's her offer? Mine's thirty days without a

drop if she's here in time for late dinner. God, only my Kate would think of -- *(suddenly stopping)* What did you just say about living down the road?

GAETANO. I hate to see my neighbors stumbling around.

HUDLEY. They wouldn't let you live on Huckleberry Drive!

GAETANO. Number 45!

HUDLEY. You're the guy in the pink house with the fountain in the driveway running twenty-four hours a day.

GAETANO. We love the sound of water. So what!

HUDLEY. And that golf green along the side made of artificial turf?

GAETANO. My handicap's down from 13 to 9.

HUDLEY. We had a monthly meeting about you last year. We almost asked you to leave. I always see your daughter playing badminton on the front lawn. She waddles. She's a blimp.

GAETANO. That blimp's my son!

(Car horn again heard honking.)

GAETANO. Ready to roll?

HUDLEY. Where are we going?

GAETANO. I already told you.

HUDLEY. Tell me again.

GAETANO. Yankee Stadium.

HUDLEY. While I think it over, kiss me on the lips.

GAETANO. What?

HUDLEY. On your knees, lick my toes.

GAETANO. Up yours!

HUDLEY. Beg me. Plead. Show me how bad you want me.

GAETANO. I've worked very hard to get this high up. Unnecessary pain upsets me. You don't have to be a drunk. You don't have to die. There are better ways to get attention.

HUDLEY. It obviously worked on you.

GAETANO. Now listen, Hud --

HUDLEY. Name's Hudley. Hudley T. Singleton, III.

GAETANO. Hudley, listen --

HUDLEY. You come over here telling me how to live with a blimp that's not even your daughter and a house that makes everyone puke and on top of that you're so stupid you can't even get my name right?!! That's three strikes. Pal, you're out. *(pointing toward door)* Out of my house, *NOW*! *(pushing GAETANO toward door)* You're starting to smell up my kitchen, *GET OUT*!!

GAETANO. Hudley, watch those hands!

HUDLEY. I was a collegiate boxing champion. Undefeated. *(assuming boxing stance)* Don't try me!

GAETANO. *(Bursts out laughing. Suddenly he dashes out kitchen door, does mocking imitation of HUDLEY.) "I was a collegiate boxing champion. Undefeated. Don't try me!" (waving down driveway, yelling)* Junior, bring the polaroid, quick! *(addressing HUDLEY through screen door)* You're funny. You're a real joker. I gotta get a shot of that, you raising your hands to me. *(yelling down driveway to son)* What do you mean, you left the polaroid with your mother? Cameras confuse her. *(He starts back into kitchen.)*

(HUDLEY crosses to cabinet, takes vodka out of hiding, gulps down a double.)

GAETANO. *(He enters, crosses to Yankee jacket on floor, picks it up, holds up jacket to HUDLEY.)* It's your last chance the easy way.

(HUDLEY grabs jacket, rips it in half, throws it to floor, takes huge gulp of vodka. GAETANO smiles. HUDLEY picks up jacket, rubs groin with it, throws back on floor, jumps on it, takes another big swig of vodka.)

GAETANO. It's good to stop a whole day before you go in.

HUDLEY. Go in where?

GAETANO. The first week you'll hate it, but by the end you won't want to leave. Pull anything you want. They've seen it all. What a place! What a view!! Nothing but picture windows!!! Tomorrow's the big day. Have everything packed.

HUDLEY. *(Suddenly spits spray of vodka in GAETANO'S face.)* I baptize you in the futility of the chase. I don't want to be saved. I don't want to be helped.

GAETANO. 9:00. I'm always on time. Be ready. *(Exits out kitchen door.)*

HUDLEY. *(Yells after GAETANO.)* I want to sleep on my kitchen floor. I want to die on my kitchen floor. I live for blackouts. I want my life to be one dark night. No one gets close. No one gets near. This is a solo flight. *(He crosses back to kitchen table, sits, drinks.)*

GAETANO. *(Suddenly bursts back into kitchen, stands by door.)*

I almost forgot. You ever raise your hands to me or spit in my face again, I'll rip off your arm and make you eat it.

(HUDLEY rushes to counter and turns on radio. Rock Music comes up very loud. GAETANO says something but can't be heard over volume. HUDLEY prances over to GAETANO a la Jagger and makes several suggestive gestures. GAETANO exits. HUDLEY bounds into action. Dancing madly about the room, he embodies everything GAETANO suggested in first scene: leaps, stomps, wiggles. He is a great dancer. Suddenly sick from violent activity, HUDLEY turns off radio and begins vomiting into sink. GAETANO suddenly appears at window over sink, talking to HUDLEY through screen.)

GAETANO. Aren't you sick and tired of being sick and tired?

HUDLEY. *(Furious, he hurls vodka bottle at GAETANO but it smashes against frame of window. He suddenly grabs framed picture of Kate off wall, spits at it, smashes glass, begins slapping face of wife in picture. Next he hurls picture on floor and begins screaming at it.)* Spend some time on the floor. See how it feels! *(He turns radio back on.)*

(Rock music blares out.)

HUDLEY. *(He resumes his mad dancing.)* No one gets close! No one gets near! This is a solo flight.

BLACKOUT

ACT I

Scene 3

Again HUDLEY T. SINGLETON, III'S kitchen. It is Wednesday, 9A.M., the following day.

Lights up! HUDLEY in bathrobe and pajamas bending over sink. He moans, shivers, continues to put water in face. HUDLEY turns around. A list of his injuries: right arm in bright white cast, compound fracture below elbow; sever laceration over right eye - seven stitches covered by butterfly bandage; left eye red and puffy; lower lip badly swollen; several front teeth loose. From a distance GAETANO approaches singing a cheerful song. He wears handsome three-piece suit and carries a package covered in bright red paper. Long silence...

HUDLEY. Who broke my arm?

GAETANO. Guess?

HUDLEY. What about my eye?

GAETANO. Every place you're hurting is complements of me.

HUDLEY. Why didn't you just kill me?

GAETANO. My son pulled me off.

HUDLEY. Let's hear.

GAETANO. Not this time.

HUDLEY. I got a right. Whatever I did, I did.

GAETANO. If you don't remember it, it ain't yours.

HUDLEY. Now listen you --

GAETANO. Smile. Today's the last of these kinds of days. No more "tell me what I did." No more --

HUDLEY. They're on their way. Police. Both my lawyers. Be here any minute. They'll want answers. They'll make demands. You'll have to tell them. They won't --

(GAETANO laughs.)

HUDLEY. Also my wife. She's flying back. She's in the air right now. Kate's agreed to give it one more try. She knows how hard I'm trying.

GAETANO. Who told her?

HUDLEY. Actually --

GAETANO. Where'd she call from?

HUDLEY. As a matter of fact --

GAETANO. All you got is me, Pal. Me and Junior and as of today, Carmella. Mrs. Good Guy's joined the club. Last night she finally confessed.

HUDLEY. Hold it? What's Carmella --

GAETANO. We drop you off at the emergency room. Me and Junior walk through the door. Carmella's sitting there, her bad leg propped up. She only needed two stitches. Both eyes'll be as good as new. Lungs too. They got all the water out in time.

HUDLEY. Is that what I did? Hurt her? Tell me. I have a right to last night. Give it back. It's mine.

GAETANO. Junior limps over, hugs her. Says, "Ma, maybe me and Dad better stop with this guy." "Nope," says she back, "we're sticking through." I scream out,

"What's this *WE* crap?" She smiles and says, "All the time you and Junior have been watching him, I've been watching you and Junior."

HUDLEY. Buddy, you don't lie very well yourself.

GAETANO. That's exactly what Junior said to Carmella. That's when she pulls out these shots she took with my polaroid of the whole striptease you pulled yesterday in the late afternoon at *THE NAUTILUS.* Man, she got you from some strange angles.

HUDLEY. What striptease?

GAETANO. Turns out she was over in the dark corner in sunglasses and a wig. Junior says, "Ma, why?" She laughs, "Whatever makes you two finally act like a father and son, I had to check out." Carmella begins to laugh. I laugh. Junior laughs. It's the first time we've laughed together since *GODFATHER II.* I break out a whole bottle of champagne. Even Junior has a taste. Carmella offers the toast, "To the sick sad guy who lives at 77 Huckleberry, we at 45 say 'Lets make him healthy and happy' "!

HUDLEY. I don't want to hear this. Get out.

GAETANO. That's only the beginning. You even turned Carmella into an affectionate woman.

HUDLEY. Maybe she'd like to see me naked? *(Starts to open robe.)* That'd really get her affections going!

(GAETANO calmly pulls gun on HUDLEY.)

HUDLEY. O God! Just what I've been waiting for!

GAETANO. I'm not going to kill you. I'll shoot your ankles off. Then your hands. Then your knees. Then your tongue. The only thing I'll leave is your ears. You'll get smaller and smaller, but you'll never die and you'll have to keep listening.

(HUDLEY laughs. GAETANO pulls back hammer. We hear a very loud click.)

GAETANO. Like I said, you've turned Carmella into an affectionate woman. After the champagne toast, Carmella tucks in Junior and goes off to sleep. She has her own bedroom. It's been that way for years. The pulling back. The more I push, the more she pulls back. In the beginning it drove me crazy. I blew up her Cadillac. I ate her favorite dress. But then I learned from it. God had sent Carmella to be my test. Nobody else can tell you that you exist. I had been trying to have Carmella tell me. A woman can't be your mirror. You can't live off somebody else's eyes. I began to back off. If she was in the living room reading and I was in the kitchen, I didn't have to keep yelling, "How's the book going?" I gave up calling home from the tennis courts to tell her I was on the way. I'm on my way. I'm getting there. I know it. She knows it. We'll still be together at the end of the day. She's the one person I don't take an edge on. Three different times she's walked on me. Every time I've gone to my knees and gotten up a bigger person. Carmella's generous and giving and wonderful but it's always been impossible for her to be affectionate. No touches. No hugs. No kisses on the neck. In twenty-two years she's never touched me first. Twenty-two years. I always have to touch her first. Sometimes she smiles and loosens up and we hug and get on with it. Other times she stiffens up. Until last night!! I jump into bed. Turn out the light. Ten minutes, my door squeaks open and she crawls in next to me. "I miss it. Want to?" I'm in shock. Next she bites my neck. Starts licking my ear. Boy, did we get on with it. We're no spring chickens, but what coos, what chirps! This morning we both wake up at the same time. I make the bed. She takes a quick shower. Hand in hand we go down to the kitchen. Junior's already got the water on for the coffee. We sit down. We talk it through. Each of us has our full say. The vote is 3-to-0. We want you as our neighbor both places.

HUDLEY. What are you saying?

GAETANO. I've just built a new summer place up in Canaan, Conneticut. Don't that sound like class itself? "Canaan, Conneticut!" Anyway, we want to build you a new summer place next to ours. All you've got to do is go in and get yourself straightened out.

HUDLEY. I don't want to hear this kind of talk. Why do you keep talking this kind of talk? This is not what I want from you.

GAETANO. Spell it out. You're educated. Form a sentence.

HUDLEY. I want to die and you won't let me.

GAETANO. Say that again.

HUDLEY. I want to die and you won't help me.

GAETANO. *(handing gun to HUDLEY)* Do it, Wasp.

HUDLEY. You think I'm scared?

GAETANO. Put it to your head. *(He helps HUDLEY put gun to temple.)* If you really want to die, die like a man. Stop with the boy-ass. Pull the trigger.

(HUDLEY finally puts finger in trigger.)

GAETANO. *(Jumps back.)* Hold it!

HUDLEY. What's wrong?

GAETANO. Aim toward the sink. I don't want any blood on my new suit.

HUDLEY. You're sick.

GAETANO. Just pull the trigger.

HUDLEY. Here, you shoot me. *(handing gun back to GAETANO)*

GAETANO. Hudley, you're one of the most interesting frauds who ever came along, but that's all you are. A fraud. A sneak. A liar. A phony and a fake.

(Suddenly a car horn honks outside. GAETANO puts gun away. HUDLEY jumps to feet.)

HUDLEY. I'm needed down at *THE NAUTILUS.* They can't open the doors unless I'm there. *THE NAUTILUS* needs me. I need *THE NAUTILUS.* I stand out. Even after I die, I'll still be there. I'm the chairman of the new softball team. I'm going to teach all the drunks how to play. We're going to drink only beer the day before the game. We're calling ourselves *THE REEF ROAD RIPPERS.* We're entered in the Bridgeport Senior Men's Slow Pitch League. Watch for us. We won't lose many. I love my new life. Something different every day. I am among friends. We've never been part of your world. We're a select few. You ought to hear our conversations. They're deep. They're clear. We cry. We laugh. We hug. We make your nights bright. We give you boring people something to ponder all day. They need me right now. I'm needed by the needy. I'm a desperado's desperado. I make life happen! You watch it go by!! *(Gives GAETANO the finger, starts out kitchen door.)* Stay out of *THE NAUTILUS.* Your kind ain't welcome. *(Exits in bathrobe. Starts down driveway, stops in shock, races back into kitchen.)* Who are all those men standing around my car?

GAETANO. They're the guys who have been watching you. They've got polaroids. Cassettes of stuff I missed. They're coming along. We're all going to explain the sort of stuff you've been pulling. It's part of the first day.

HUDLEY. *(screaming out kitchen door)* I'm not going in. Hey, Greasers, I'm not going in. Get in here. You're going to have to kill me.

GAETANO. *(Tears open the red present. It's a long, white jacket.)* Put this on.

HUDLEY. Come again?

GAETANO. *(throwing white jacket to HUDLEY)* It's a jacket of surrender. They won't admit you without it.

HUDLEY. You mustn't do this to me. I need some time. How about tomorrow? Today's too soon.

(GAETANO shakes head "NO".)

HUDLEY. O.K., today; but only if you find Kate. You don't have to drag her back here. Get her on the phone. Show me her voice. Let me hear her say, "If you'll go in, I'll come back."

(GAETANO starts to help HUDLEY into jacket.)

HUDLEY. I want last night back. You took it, Robber. Give it back, *now. (He suddenly gives GAETANO a hard elbow in stomach.)* I'm kicking your ass, Dago! *(Steps back, throws jacket at GAETANO.)*

GAETANO. You're a cripple. I can't put a beating on a cripple.

HUDLEY. It didn't stop you last night! *(raising hands, starting to feint and move)* I'll start off by cutting you above both eyes. Round two, I'll work down to the body. You'll be bent over like a meatball. Olive oil coming out of you everywhere. Round three, I charge --

(Suddenly GAETANO charges, throwing a wild right that HUDLEY easily slips. GAETANO turns, his hands held low. GAETANO starts to step inside to throw body blow, but HUDLEY stings him with three crisp, hard jabs with good left hand. HUDLEY backs and circles, GAETANO chases. GAETANO jabs weak and short and is caught by solid left hook from HUDLEY. GAETANO instinctively reaches to face, discovers blood.)

HUDLEY. One arm and I'm turning you into a pizza pie. Wait till they hear about this at *THE NAUTILUS.* I'll recreate this beating every Monday morning. We'll put up a crepe paper ring. We'll find some punched-up Greaser to play you.

GAETANO. You're going in.

HUDLEY. You're going down.

GAETANO. I'm dragging you through the door.

HUDLEY. They'll drag you out of the ring.

(GAETANO roars once, roars twice, picks up pace. GAETANO chases HUDLEY around room, hoping to land one big K.O. punch ... as HUDLEY, schooled and talented, turns GAETANO'S face into a bloody mess. Suddenly HUDLEY

stops on a dime, sets feet wide for power ... as one of GAETANO'S wild hooks lands flush and knocks HUDLEY to the floor, unconscious. GAETANO picks up white jacket, stands HUDLEY up, puts jacket on him and then throws him over shoulder. Exit GAETANO out door with HUDLEY. Screen door slams. Lights slowly fade.)

END OF ACT ONE

ACT II
Scene 1

Again HUDLEY T. SINGLETON, III'S kitchen. Three months have passed. The week between Christmas and New Year's. It is Thursday, 2P.M.

Lights up! Big changes in the kitchen. Refrigerator has been repositioned. Liquor cabinet is gone. Rest of the cabinets have been stripped and painted a new color. The kitchen table is a stunning colonial antique. Tile floor is covered with a thick, soft rug. Over the door has been hung a sign:

WELCOME HOME
HERO!!

Several seconds and voices are heard. HUDLEY appears first, followed by GAETANO, carrying suitcases. HUDLEY holds door, GAETANO enters with suitcases, sets them center of the room and quickly sits at table. Enter HUDLEY. He carries "white coat of surrender" over his arm. He stops at door and looks at changes in kitchen. Slowly, he starts way around room, touching, smelling, studying additions very closely. It is almost unbearable the time he takes...

GAETANO. Say you like it. I busted my hump.
HUDLEY. Why'd you do it?

GAETANO. "Purposeful change."

HUDLEY. Come again?

GAETANO. Almost all the books stressed it. Get rid of this. Move that. Try the new. Go with the different. As I think one Dr. Vernon E. Johnson so aptly put it in his now-legendary book, *I'll Quit Tomorrow*, "If the recovering person returns to find an air of purposeful change, his chances of recovery are greatly enhanced."

HUDLEY. Gaetano, your vocabulary's expanding.

GAETANO. I've read a lot, Pal. A ton of words getting ready for you. Thirty-nine books I went through. Got blisters turning pages. I used to be smart about you. Now I'm brilliant. Ain't nothing you can pull that I ain't read up on. Square business. Hudley, can you or can't you?

HUDLEY. Can I or can't I what?

GAETANO. Feel the air of purposeful change!

HUDLEY. Very definitely.

GAETANO. Off with your shoes!

HUDLEY. Beg pardon?

GAETANO. You ain't even got laces. Kick 'em off.

(HUDLEY kicks off "Penny Loafers" and stands at attention.)

GAETANO. Now go for a walk across your new rug!

(As HUDLEY crosses rug in socks...)

GAETANO. Warm and cosy and cuddly, right?

HUDLEY. Very definitely.

GAETANO. This used to be a cold kitchen. Now it's warm and cosy and cuddly. That, my friend, is "purposeful change!" *(He suddenly grabs HUDLEY'S loafers, crosses to sink, opens door, and tosses loafers into the garbage can.)*

HUDLEY. Those are my favorite shoes!!

GAETANO. Brand new pair upstairs, Pal.

HUDLEY. *WHAT?!!*

GAETANO. Go look in your closet. Everything's brand new. Shirts. Jackets. Pants. Even the ties.

HUDLEY. But I love to wear clothes that are old and lived in.

GAETANO. Read a whole book about holding on to the old. Those days are over. Off with your pants!

HUDLEY. *WHAT?!!*

GAETANO. They're old. They're going in the trash.

(HUDLEY takes off his pants, hands them to GAETANO.)

GAETANO. Shirt too!

(HUDLEY takes off his shirt, hands it to GAETANO.)

GAETANO. Go see your closet. Smile, Pal, welcome to the new.

(In underwear, HUDLEY starts to exit.)

GAETANO. *(Blocks him.)* How you feeling?

HUDLEY. Fine.

GAETANO. The truth!

HUDLEY. I want to tear out your goddamn eyes.

GAETANO. From now on, that's the new rule around here: Say what you feel the minute you feel it.

HUDLEY. You're going to drive me goddamn crazy!

GAETANO. Whatever it takes, Hud, whatever it takes!!

(HUDLEY exits upstairs.)

GAETANO. *(He throws pants and shirt in garbage. Quickly he crosses to door leading upstairs.)* Here's a song I made up for you. It's called *"Hud, You're My Bud". (loudly singing up stairwell)*

WHEN YOU LEFT A SHORT THREE MONTHS AGO,
WAS THE ONLY WAY TO STOP YOU KNOW
YOU WERE IN DETOX, BOY, WAS I LOW
GET UP IN THE MORNING, NOWHERE TO GO
THEN I STARTED WHISPERIN' REAL SLOW
IN A VOICE REAL ITALIAN AND LOW
HUD, YOU'RE MY BUD, SPIT OUT THAT CRUD
LET'S GET HEALTHY, LET'S GET WEALTHY
HUD, YOU'RE MY BUD, SPIT OUT THAT--

(Enter HUDLEY in beautifully tailored new pants, buttoning beautifully tailored new shirt.)

HUDLEY. They would get us up at dawn and make us do sit-ups together. At all the different meetings and lectures we would have to sit together. Even if we weren't hungry, we still had to go to meals and all sit together. If you couldn't sleep, if your feelings were stuck, if your pain didn't feel right, you call a meeting no matter what time it was and talk it out together. Your group is your life. Alone, you're dead. Finally, last week I accepted. I hated every minute of it. I wanted to kill, hurt, maim, scream, jump out of my skin. One single thought kept me going: Wait till Kate sees what I've done to myself. Every night, going to sleep, I'd run a movie through my mind. I walk through that back door, I put down those bags, I run up those stairs and find her in bed, waiting for me. Well, I just found her waiting for me in bed!!

GAETANO. *WHAT?!!*

HUDLEY. Not exactly waiting but she's here. I mean, she's here but she's not here right now. She's definitely been here recently. The bed's still warm.

GAETANO. Hud, listen--

HUDLEY. She's probably out running. She loves to run. She has the legs of a dancer. She'll be back any minute. Kate hates being hugged when she's sweaty. I'll just give her a kiss on the cheek. I'll sit on my bed. I'll listen to the shower go. I'll hear the water hitting her. I find that incredibly sexy: listening to water hit someone you love. After that, I'll dry her off with her big red towel. It doesn't always lead to something, but touching her like that, the circular rubbing, well--

GAETANO. Kate's not here.

HUDLEY. Once she's dressed, we'll go for a drive up north. They'll be snow everywhere. Kids dragging their sleds, chimneys smoking, old -- *(suddenly stopping)* What did you *just* say?!!

GAETANO. Kate's not here.

HUDLEY. Who's been sleeping in her bed?

GAETANO. I didn't make it this morning. I was real late.

HUDLEY. Late for what?

GAETANO. Picking you up. Danny Wheels' son had Little League Hockey practice at nine. After that we had to --

HUDLEY. I don't want to hear that *you've* been sleeping in her bed. I want to hear that *she's* been sleeping in her bed. Has she called?

GAETANO. Once.

HUDLEY. Did she ask how I was doing? Was she happy to hear?

GAETANO. Danny Wheels was doing the cabinets. He took the call.

HUDLEY. How long ago? A week? A month? Yesterday?

GAETANO. Hudley, look at me.

HUDLEY. Something's wrong! Tell me what's wrong!!

GAETANO. I've been on it since you went in. We're working on it! We're working on it!!

HUDLEY. *WORK HARDER!* She's got to be here now. I'm ready to roll. *(taking out a piece of paper)* I even drew up a list of resolutions. She loves lists of resolutions. Katy, here's mine! *One,* when I get too needy, go for a walk. *Two,* when she gets withdrawn, make sure I let her sleep alone. *Three... Three... (He begins to cry.)* I have a clear plan. I see a bright future. I've worked so hard to turn myself around. I've got to have her here now. The pictures in my mind aren't going to go away. I'm always going to see us together. Haven't I earned even a little chance? *(He covers face with hands.)* That's all I did in there. I'm so tired of crying. I didn't think I had any left.

(GAETANO hands him a handkerchief.)

HUDLEY. Thanks.

GAETANO. Silk. There's a dozen more in your drawer upstairs next to your socks. They're initialled too. HTS,III.

HUDLEY. Katey loves monogrammed handkerchiefs. I remember one time for Christmas she got me six --

GAETANO. The first week I'll be the one to get up early.

HUDLEY. For a few days I want to be by myself.

GAETANO. No way! All the books say the first three months are the worst time to be alone. You leave your recovery to the man who's looked into it. O.K., so the first week I get you up. Lead you to the shower. We'll keep up this exercise business. We'll do sit-ups together, jumping jacks, two-three rounds of light sparring. Talk together, go for walks together. Eat. Sleep. Dream. Everything together. We'll be out here just like you were in there!

HUDLEY. *(mocking imitation)* "WE'LL BE OUT HERE JUST LIKE YOU WERE IN THERE!" That means every day the first week you want me to get on my knees and tell you how much I need you? That means every day the first week I must crawl and say out loud three times that I cannot do it alone?! Do I have to scream it?! Do I have to moan?! Must I write every morning on the bathroom mirror the number of drinks I had in my dreams?!! That was the way it was in there. Is that how you want it out here? You going to threaten me if I go to the bathroom without my slippers? You going to send me to bed if I--

(GAETANO suddenly starts laughing.)

HUDLEY. Do you always laugh at sick people?

GAETANO. Three different books said laughter was the great way to welcome the recovering person home.

HUDLEY. I don't want to hear about any more books! All I want is --

GAETANO. Laughter and a nice big hug. How about a nice big hug? *(He opens arms to HUDLEY.)*

(HUDLEY doesn't move.)

GAETANO. Hudley, my arms are waiting.

(Still HUDLEY doesn't move.)

GAETANO. Hudley, my arms are getting pissed off!

(HUDLEY crosses slowly to GAETANO, the two men hug each other.)

GAETANO. Welcome home, Hero.

HUDLEY. I may need a lot of this.

GAETANO. Whatever it takes, Hud, whatever it takes.

BLACKOUT

ACT II
Scene2

Again HUDLEY T. SINGLETON III'S kitchen. It is the following day, Friday, 9 A.M.

Lights up! HUDLEY is preparing breakfast in kitchen area. HUDLEY wears apron over Santa Claus red pants and Santa Claus black boots. There is several seconds of silence, then the voice of GAETANO singing the Italian song he sang in the first scene of Act I. He enters, drying his hair with red towel, never looking at HUDLEY as he crosses to breakfast table...

GAETANO. *(sitting at table)* That was fun! Push-ups and sit-ups first thing in the morning. Usually I do my workout in the middle of the afternoon. Jog a mile. Toss up a few light weights. Bang the heavy bag. Do I love to bang the heavy bag! You ask about me down on Mulberry Street. In my day I could bang like a truck. For a few years they called me "The Truck." Entered me once in the Golden Gloves. First fight was against a Mul-On-Yom. Big as a tree. Rangy. Quick. I've always been wide and wild. That's what they started calling me after the fight. Changed my name from "The Truck" to "Wide And Wild". Anyway, the fight was in some armory uptown. I forget exactly where. My buddies from Mulberry Street were all at ringside. Smoking fat cigars, rings on their pinkies, "SQUISH THE YOM, SQUISH THE YOM". One thing about Italians. They know how to sit at ringside! O.K., round one starts and I wade in low. *(crossing to HUDLEY)* Here, you be the "Yom". *(Suddenly sees the Santa outfit.)* Hudley, what's that under your apron?

HUDLEY. In there they taught us to do one thing a day for other people. I'm going to be Santa Claus for some kids in Bridgeport.

GAETANO. It's almost New Year's.

HUDLEY. These kids are retarded. They're happy to see Santa anytime.

GAETANO. I played Santa once. Fact is it's how I met Carmella.

HUDLEY. *(stirring eggs on stove)* You keep calling for her i your sleep. *(imitating GAETANO)* "CARMELLA?! CARMELLA?!!"

GAETANO. She's in Miami. Her mother's not well. Been gone since just after you went in. If she hadn't been called away, she definitely would've helped me with your kitchen. A lot of what I did, I got from calling her on the phone. I don't really deserve her. I hope she never figures it out.

HUDLEY. Drink your coffee. It's getting cold.

GAETANO. *(sipping from cup in front of him)* My son'll be coming by a little later.

HUDLEY. What's he been up to?

GAETANO. He was staying in your bed till yesterday. Some job he did taking your place! Shovelling snow, hanging storm windows. Several times we drove out to Jersey and watched you through that bay window eat dinner.

HUDLEY. How's he doing with the weight?

GAETANO. 107 pounds. 47 more and he'll be below 200. Now that you can see his face, the girls are starting to call. If they get him hot before he's ready, I'll kill every one of them.

(HUDLEY crosses to table with two omelettes in pan, serving first GAETANO, then himself.)

GAETANO. I don't eat omelettes.

HUDLEY. It's mushroom and mozzerella. Give it a try.

(GAETANO starts to eat with a fork; HUDLEY grabs it out of his hand.)

HUDLEY. Hold it!

GAETANO. What's wrong?

HUDLEY. First drink your juice.

GAETANO. I don't drink juice.

HUDLEY. You do if you live with me. Drink, Italian.

(GAETANO drinks juice.)

HUDLEY. Squeezed it just for you. *(He hands fork back to GAETANO.)*

GAETANO. *(Eats omelette.)* Where'd you learn to cook like this?

HUDLEY. I always make breakfast for Kate.

GAETANO. *(taking bite from English muffin)* Muffin's great too.

HUDLEY. I broil them already buttered. Makes all the difference.

GAETANO. I'm impressed. This is one tremendous muffin.

HUDLEY. Wait till you see what I've got cooking for dinner. *(Bursts out laughing.)* Fact is I cook most of the meals. My specialty is dinner parties of ten or more. The only thing we agreed that I could do better than Kate was cook. There wasn't a goddamn thing we could do together that was fun and easy. Who's turn it was to take out the garbage was a world war. As for sex ---, well, our life in bed was so complicated --- who leads, who follows, who should've spent more time on what, "DONE THERE, MOVE ON," her always screaming "ONLY THE TIP, ONLY THE TIP!"

GAETANO. What tip? Tip of what?

HUDLEY. If we were both hot, fine! But if one was and the other wasn't - she used to leave notes on the bathroom mirror, "Tonight's your turn to lead off!"

GAETANO. There's too much talk about sex. It's a silent activity.

HUDLEY. What do you mean, "silent activity."

GAETANO. A good lover is like a submarine. Run silent. Run deep.

HUDLEY. *(laughing)* "RUN SILENT? RUN DEEP?"

GAETANO. Shut up! I know sex. Wanna hear who I've slept with in Vegas? I've made show girls give up dancing. I once got a Chinese girl to put on a Yankee cap. I've made women of seven different nations moan. My record speaks for itself. I've put in my time. Step to step. No talking. You can't miss if you follow the Italian method.

HUDLEY. One time I got so mad at Kate, I screamed, "IT'S NOT ME WHO COMES TOO EARLY. IT'S YOU WHO COME'S TOO LATE!"

GAETANO. *(spitting out food)* Hud, do you mind?! I'm trying to eat.

HUDLEY. No two human beings were ever more uncomfortable with each other. I think that's why she picked me. Cause she knew we could never be close. The distance made me crazy and made her feel safe. Today you hear all this crap about intimacy? I don't believe it! Most couples pick each other so there can be that little distance. I was always trying to speak up. "KATE, I THINK THE WALL BETWEEN US SUCKS. WHATAYA SAY WE SMASH IT DOWN?"

GAETANO. Hud, can we please just --

HUDLEY. When I think of us, that's what I see: a wall with us on either side. The thing I hated most was how I was always trying to get her to smile. As long as I keep her smiling, at least she won't take off. Always worrying about how to keep someone from leaving is so --

GAETANO. Hudley!

HUDLEY. How can I know what I do and miss her so much? If she walked through the door right now, I'd --*(He puts face in hands.)*

(GAETANO continues eating.)

HUDLEY. *(Sits up, resumes eating.)* Pass the salt.

GAETANO. *(passing salt)* Hudley, know what I'm going to do for you? If you make 90 days, I'm going to name a little league team after you. Call them *HUDLEY'S HUNGRY*

BEARS. Fairfield County needs some heros to look up to. Also, I want you to hook up with my corporation *GOOD GUY ENTERPRISES* today. Got some problems. Could use your expert touch.

HUDLEY. I already have a job. I'm president of my own little P.R. firm.

GAETANO. What did you make last year?

HUDLEY. Almost a hundred thousand.

GAETANO. Hook up with me and you'll do a quarter-of-a-million the first year. All legit. I can already see it now. Every morning we head for Manhattan, Danny behind the wheel. We plan our strategy, figure our moves. We're a born team: your education, my brains.

HUDLEY. Do you know that you're the first person I've ever enjoyed sleeping with!

GAETANO. Don't start! I got friends who wear dresses!!

HUDLEY. I've always slept in bedrooms with women. Connive my way into HER bed. Talk HER into joining me in mine. Last night it was completely different. You were over in one bed. I was in the other. We turned out the lights. You crawled out of bed. Suddenly you're on your knees praying.

GAETANO. I'm Catholic. Catholics spend a lot of time on their knees.

HUDLEY. I heard you say the words, "Dear God, most of all help Hudley make it through!!"

GAETANO. I ain't ashamed. I care.

HUDLEY. *(During speech, he removes apron, puts pillow in stomach to create belly and dons Santa coat.)* Suddenly I hear my voice say, "dear God, thanks for sending Gaetano."

I've never prayed before. I don't believe in anything. It was my first day home. I thought, "Are the miracles already starting?" Then you called out for Carmella. *(imitating GAETANO)* "Carmella, please touch me first." You shuddered. Your blanket fell off. I didn't want to move. I get up. I pick up the blanket. I put it back on you. A smile comes over your face. I go back to bed. I lie there. I look up. I say, "We're going through all these little things together. We're helping each other through the night." Yes, my friend, you are the first person I've ever enjoyed sleeping with. How about some more coffee? *(He picks up both cups, starts for sink.)*

(Car horn honks loudly.)

HUDLEY. *(Puts cups in sink.)* Get my beard and hat!

GAETANO. Where?

HUDLEY. In our bedroom.

GAETANO. *(starting off)* I'm coming along. See if you're as good at Santa Claus as I was.

HUDLEY. Also, grab the bag of presents in the front hall closet.

(Exit GAETANO down hallway. Phone rings.)

HUDLEY. *(Answers phone, talks into receiver.)* Hello? ... Yes, he's here but he's stepped out of the room for a minute --- Sure I'll take a message. What? They're flying Kate home? --- No, no, that's exactly what we've both been waiting for! *(writing on small pad)* What's the flight number again? --- When does it land? --- JFK, right --- No, no it was completely my pleasure, Pal. *(He hangs up phone.)*

GAETANO. *(Immediately enters with Santa beard and hat, bag of presents over shoulder and some of HUDLEY'S street clothes.)* Brought you a change for after so we can make a meeting on the way back from Bridgeport. *(looking at thin pamphlet of "A.A." meetings)* Danny's marked Friday for Fairfield. Do you know where North Benson Road is?

HUDLEY. *(laughing)* Thanks again!

GAETANO. What for?

HUDLEY. Flight 302!

GAETANO. Flight 302 from where?

HUDLEY. Tucson! That's where Kate - *Goddammit!! (slapping head in disgust)* Twice before she's hidden out in Tucson with that friend from Wellesley. Name of Neecy McPhee. Anyway, I'm glad your people finally found her.

GAETANO. The doctors were worried that if I told you too soon, you wouldn't be able to handle it.

HUDLEY. Handle what? My wife's flying home. My Kate's coming back to me. She'll come through the door. I'll lift her in the air. No booze on my breath. Finally she'll want to get close!

GAETANO. Buddy Pal, Kate's not coming home.

HUDLEY. Don't joke. Please.

GAETANO. It's her body. Kate's dead. She died two weeks ago yesterday.

HUDLEY. Is this some test to see if my treatment worked?

GAETANO. I couldn't tell you while you were still in. I was timing it out for today ... to tell you in time to meet the plane ... only Dom Boy in Tucson called here instead of --

HUDLEY. Who killed her?

GAETANO. She drowned in her girlfriend's pool.

HUDLEY. She's a great swimmer. Great swimmers don't die swimming in swimming pools.

GAETANO. No one's sure what happened. Her girlfriend was on the phone. When she got back, Kate was at the bottom of the pool.

HUDLEY. This sort of thing doesn't happen to people like me. *(Smashes both cups in sink.)* I've gotten myself all turned around. Healthy. *(Smashes everything off the kitchen table.)* I've got a happy ending all planned out. She'll come through the door. I'll lift her in the air. No booze on my ... no booze .... *(Sits at kitchen table.)* Tell me once more.

GAETANO. Kate's dead. She's not coming home.

HUDLEY. Again!

GAETANO. Kate's dead. She's not coming home.

HUDLEY. Just heard my wife died and I can't even cry. People are supposed to cry at times like these.

GAETANO. Forget "suppose". Say what you feel.

HUDLEY. Know what I really feel? Free! Tell me it's not sick to feel free. I need to know my feelings aren't sick. I'm going to throw up.

GAETANO. Go ahead.

HUDLEY. Make her come back.

GAETANO. How?

HUDLEY. Let her come through that door so I can lift her in the air.

GAETANO. I can't do that.

HUDLEY. Do something. I can't do anything. I can't

move. I can't feel. I can't think. I'm dead inside. She's better off. She's dead all over.

GAETANO. Take a breath.

HUDLEY. But --

GAETANO. Take one!

(HUDLEY takes first breath.)

GAETANO. Another!

(HUDLEY takes second.)

GAETANO. One more!

(HUDLEY takes third.)

GAETANO. Now do the first thing that comes to mind!

HUDLEY. *(He grabs beard and hat from GAETANO, puts them on. Next he grabs up bag of presents and throws over shoulder.)* Those kids are waiting for Christmas. *(Starts for door, bursts into a sprightly Christmas song about Santa Claus.)*

(GAETANO joins in singing, races to door, opens it for HUDLEY to exit. HUDLEY starts out door, can't, tries again, can't, singing dies. HUDLEY crosses to table, sits down, takes off beard and hat, lies bag of presents at feet. GAETANO sits at table across from HUDLEY. HUDLEY lets out a loud scream. Next he reaches hand across table to GAETANO. GAETANO takes it. The two men hold hands.)

BLACKOUT

ACT II

Scene 3

Again HUDLEY T. SINGLETON III'S kitchen. A few days later, the second day of the new year. It is 2 P.M.

Lights up! No one in kitchen. Snow is falling outside window. Over chair in far corner is HUDLEY'S "white jacket of surrender". Breakfast table has been moved to center of the room. Bright tablecloth, lighted candles, but most of all, an elaborate spread of food, cheese, salami, peppers, roast beef, an Italian feast. Several seconds and GAETANO enters, followed by HUDLEY. Both wear winter coats with black armbands around arms...

HUDLEY. What's this?

GAETANO. Right now's just like back then!

HUDLEY. Back when?

GAETANO. I'd come through the door and be stunned just the way we are now. She barks out, "Your son, THE CATERER." He races on, bakers hat, big white bib, the works. I snarl, "NO SON OF MINE CATERS. HE OWNS THE STORE." *(parading around the table, pointing at individual delicacies)* Look at how that avocado's sliced. See how the prosciutto's layed out. Observe: hot peppers one end, sweet the other! Salami peeled back like a stripper. Roast beef, celery, olives. Check out that provolone. Only one person does it that way.

HUDLEY. Who?

GAETANO. Only of course it wasn't!

HUDLEY. Of course *who* wasn't?

GAETANO. The kid's too much!

HUDLEY. Too much *how?*

GAETANO. Doing the things he does to make his dad forget!

HUDLEY. Forget *what?*!

GAETANO. He did this to make me think she was back. My wife's not coming home either. Says she'd rather stay in Miami. She says, "Enough's enough!"

HUDLEY. I'm just the excuse she needed, right? People are always using me to be the excuse they need. Kate. You. Carmella. Even back at Brown it was always the same crap. My freshman year I was already the best ball-player in the whole school but --

GAETANO. Didn't my boy come through with flying colors?

HUDLEY. He doesn't even exist!

GAETANO. Your sentences sound a little off. You feeling O.K.?

HUDLEY. I feel great. I'm a widower who's tired of pretending certain things exist that don't exist. Your son does not exist. I mean, you keep saying tomorrow, tomorrow, only --

GAETANO. You met him today.

HUDLEY. When?!

GAETANO. At the cemetery! He shook your hand in the

line at the end. Gave you that big kiss on the cheek. He came after the guy with the braces.

HUDLEY. Where?!

GAETANO. In the line. During the service he was standing off to the side by himself. Black suit. White shirt. Black tie. White carnation. Class itself.

HUDLEY. The one crying? That kid making all the noise?

GAETANO. I was so proud of him. Able to let go like that. My son felt very close to Kate.

HUDLEY. When did they meet?

GAETANO. Hudley, that was some soliloquy!

HUDLEY. It's called a eulogy!

GAETANO. My son wasn't the only one crying. There were snifles all over the place. Franky Topcoat, an old and honored friend who drove all the way up from New York, was bent over like a baby. When you went on and on about not being enough to make Kate happy, I thought he was going to fall on his face.

HUDLEY. Do you think we could --

GAETANO. Danny Wheels taped the whole thing. I got a copy in my pocket. We pop it in the machine and you can hear for yourself. You were moving. You were open. You touched many different hearts.

HUDLEY. Could you please tell me why you're doing all this?

GAETANO. Fact is this guy Franky Topcoat brought along from New York, name of Tommy the Grip, he's in video, -- well, through the window of Franky Topcoat's limosine this Tommy the Grip shoots the whole scene with this incredibly long lens that makes your face look no more than two feet away. Close enough to see what your skin's thinking. This particular lens Tommy the Grip had in today is called "The Eye Of Truth"!

HUDLEY. All right! Enough!! Stop!!!

GAETANO. Tell him. He's on his way with a Betamax!

HUDLEY. *WHAT?!!*

GAETANO. Going to show your eulogy on T.V. I want you to watch yourself. See if you get what I got. We'll all be witnessing the evidence for the second time. You, me, Danny Wheels, Franky Topcoat, Tommy the Grip, maybe my son might even find some time!

HUDLEY. Hold it! Where'd they all come from?

GAETANO. The lights'll come back on. You'll stand. You'll quiet the crowd. That's when I want you to tell them.

HUDLEY. Tell them what?

GAETANO. How you did it.

HUDLEY. Did what?

GAETANO. Gave that speech over Kate's grave in the shape you were in!

HUDLEY. I forgot my head. I listened to my heart. I felt a responsibility to the crowd. I kept telling myself "You're a widower lamenting the loss of a wife who you loved more than ... more than ..." *(suddenly cannot continue)* Who meant more to me than ... than ...

GAETANO. Hud, you're a sneak!

HUDLEY. I also kept telling myself that my heart --

GAETANO. Hud, you're a liar!

HUDLEY. Every word out of my mouth I was aware that my heart --

GAETANO. Hud, you're a phoney and a fake!

HUDLEY. She was lying there and my heart --

GAETANO. *(suddenly grabbing HUDLEY by collar)* Look at me, Hud!

HUDLEY. *(faces inches apart)* I'm looking!

GAETANO. Danny Wheels' mother with the spaghetti was sad, but today was mean!

HUDLEY. Mean how?!

GAETANO. Ask Kate!

HUDLEY. She's gone.

GAETANO. She's back for a quick visit!

(Suddenly GAETANO grabs chair by table and hurls it to the center of the room. GAETANO grabs HUDLEY; both men are before the chair. GAETANO gestures as though Kate were there.)

GAETANO. She's listening. Ask her.

HUDLEY. Ask her *what*?

GAETANO. How it felt hearing her eulogy being delivered by a drunk?

HUDLEY. I'm not drunk. I only took a few to brace myself.

GAETANO. Don't tell me. Tell her. Say, "Kate, I'm not drunk. I only took a few to brace myself."

HUDLEY. Kate, I'm not ... I'm not ...

GAETANO. She's all ears. Spill it.

HUDLEY. Kate, I am drunk. Been sneaking for almost two days. All the old tricks. The breath mints. The talking out of the side of my mouth. The hiding. The sneaking.

GAETANO. Hand it over.

(HUDLEY reaches into pocket and takes out half-empty pint of vodka. He hands it over to GAETANO.)

GAETANO. *(Gestures toward chair.)* She can't stay long. Tell her.

HUDLEY. Kate, listen -- We played all these games in there.

GAETANO. I'm not playing games, Pal. I'll walk out that door. I'll leave you alone. I'll seal this house off! You'll get your air through little holes!!

HUDLEY. I said everything I had to say at the grave.

GAETANO. That was the nice stuff. The way you wanted it. What you needed people to hear. We want the real stuff, right, Katey? Gutsball. Once and for all. Look at her laughing at you!

HUDLEY. Where?

GAETANO. Katey says you lost your guts years ago.

HUDLEY. Where were yours, you bitch, when you went under in that pool! *(Attacks chair, screaming at it, hitting it, knocking it over. Through the speech it becomes Kate.)* When you drowned, you took my stomach, my heart. What am I supposed to do now? You're all I've been waiting for. Gaetano, why did we wait so --

GAETANO. Not me! Her!!

HUDLEY. *(back to addressing chair)* Why did we wait so long? Why did we let it get so late? Why did we let that wall get so high? For about a month almost two years ago, I almost found the courage to come and talk to you but those one or two extra vodkas on the train made talking unnecessary. Look at what all the waiting got us. You're dead and I'm a drunk. Why couldn't I have once during all those years taken you aside and told you how disappointed I was. How scared I'd gotten. Ask how you felt. Were you stricken with fear too? If you came back right now, that's what I'd say. "Kate, I know I can never be great, but is it O.K.? Is it something you can live with? If we talk about it enough, is it something we can live with? I don't wan't to be average but I am and that's it." Please come back for a minute and tell me what you'd say back if I told you my fears. *(shaking chair)* If I drove you away, I can make you come back. *(hitting chair)* Come back, come back, come back! *(Stops hitting, stands up.)* I don't want to be alone anymore. I need someone to hold me.

GAETANO. Ask.

HUDLEY. Hold me.

(GAETANO holds HUDLEY. There is a long silence. GAETANO steps back.)

HUDLEY. What am I going to do? What am I going to do?

GAETANO. Start all over again.

HUDLEY. Start *WHAT* all over again?

GAETANO. Pal, you're going back in!

HUDLEY. Tell me this time I'll make it.

GAETANO. I can't.

HUDLEY. You've read all the books. Tell me something I can hold on to.

(Suddenly GAETANO hugs HUDLEY while also holding him in the air. GAETANO lets HUDLEY down to the floor.)

HUDLEY. When do I go?

GAETANO. Danny Wheels is waiting outside.

HUDLEY. What about packing my bags?

GAETANO. Already in the trunk of the limo.

HUDLEY. How did you know all along I'd be going back in?

GAETANO. Some Italians know certain things.

HUDLEY. Will you be here when I get back?

(GAETANO lowers his head.)

HUDLEY. Gaetano, are you crying?

GAETANO. Do you see them?

HUDLEY. Touch your eyes.

GAETANO. I can feel them running down.

HUDLEY. You must be my friend. A big guy like you crying over saying good-by to me.

GAETANO. Screw you, Wasp. It's me I'm worried about. *(Takes out handkerchief, blows nose.)* Wife of twenty years gone.

HUDLEY. You got your son. At least --

GAETANO. How long's that gonna last? Every day more girls calling. I keep worrying I finally did something right in my life and I'm going to end up alone. Know what I'd like from you?

HUDLEY. What?

GAETANO. Say it.

HUDLEY. Say what?

GAETANO. For the right reason this time.

HUDLEY. For the right reason this time.

GAETANO. No expecting me here.

HUDLEY. No expecting Gaetano here.

GAETANO. No doing it to show someone else.

HUDLEY. No doing it to show someone else.

GAETANO. Take care of your life so I can start taking care of mine.

HUDLEY. Take care of my life so Gaetano can start taking care of his.

(The two men embrace, laugh, pull apart.)

GAETANO. Tell you one thing. I'm going to stay around here long enough to change this kitchen again. 'Purposeful change" is the key. "Purposeful change" till the day we die. This time I'll take the style more in the colonial direction. After that, I'd like to ---

(suddenly from outside, the sound of a car horn honking)

HUDLEY. Don't stop. Tell me more.

GAETANO. We'll start off by painting the house a new color. White isn't you. Next, we'll build a rock garden.

HUDLEY. Where?

GAETANO. Out under the birch tree where the grass doesn't grow.

HUDLEY. What about my Little League team. "Hudley's Hungry Bears". Can I coach third and wave my little guys home?

GAETANO. We can wave to each other. I'll be over at first.

HUDLEY. I'll go back to batting clean-up on the firehouse team. I'll blast it over everyone's head. Don't stop. Tell me more.

(Another car horn honking. GAETANO gets jacket of surrender, crosses back to HUDLEY, puts it over his shoulders.)

HUDLEY. If I go out that door, I'll die.

(GAETANO leads HUDLEY through door.)

HUDLEY. I didn't die.

(Lights slowly descend as HUDLEY and GAETANO disappear down path to driveway.)

END OF PLAY

COSTUME PLOT

HUDLEY

I-1 Red boxer shorts (worn throughout)
Wrinkled trousers, shirt, vest, tie

I-2 same as I-1

I-3 Brown bathrobe (ripped sleeve)
Cast and sling
Face bandage
Blue slippers
White coat of surrender

II-1 Corduroy trousers
Plaid shirt
Down jacket
Loafers
Blue crepe de chine shirt
Black trousers
Black shoes

II-2 White undershirt
Red corduroy Santa pants
Santa boot tops
Red and blue apron
Black shoes
Glasses
Santa jacket, beard, hat

II-3 Dark brown suit
Belt
Beige shirt
Tie
Black overcoat
White coat of surrender

GAETANO

I-1 Blue pinstripe trousers with suspenders
Blue patterned silk shirt
Tie
Blue trenchcoat
Lavender handkerchief
Black shoes
Dark blue hat

I-2 Altobelli Enterprises baseball shirt
Red baseball trousers
White tassel pumps
Red baseball cap
Spikes and glove

I-3 Grey suit jacket
Grey suit trousers
Orange and grey striped shirt
Orange tie and clip
Shoulder holster and gun
Grey hat
Black shoes

II-1 Tan trousers
Brown argyle sweater
Handkerchief (monogrammed "H")
Black shoes

II-2 Jogging suit
Red towel
Blue wool overcoat with fur collar
White shoes

II-3 Blue pinstripe trousers with suspenders
Blue pinstripe vest and jacket
White shirt
Burgundy tie
Blue wool overcoat with fur collar
Black shoes
White silk scarf
Dark blue hat

PROP LIST

I-1 Red wrapped package containing
cassette player and cassette tape
Red boxer shorts
Kitchen table dressing
Styrofoam coffee cup with coffee
Money
Cabinet dressing
Wall phone
Paper towels on rack
Dish cloth
Brown University official transcript
Milk carton
Refrigerator dressing

I-2 First base softball glove
Fielders softball glove
Softball
Altobelli Enterprises "Big Hud" baseball shirt
Vodka bottle

I-3 Red wrapped package containing
White coat of surrender (costume)
Gun in shoulder holster (costume)
Bridgeport Post sports section
Vodka bottle

II-1 Suitcase
Garbage can
Handkerchief (costume)
Sign - WELCOME HOME HERO
Wallet
List of resolutions

II-2 Frying pan
Mixing bowls and utensils
Dishes and glasses
Napkins
Muffins, eggs, juice
Toaster oven
Bag of presents
Box with Santa jacket, belt, beard, hat, pillow
Phone notepad and pen

II-3 Italian buffet plate
Candles
Table cloth
Utensils, plates, napkins
Coat of surrender
Vodka bottle

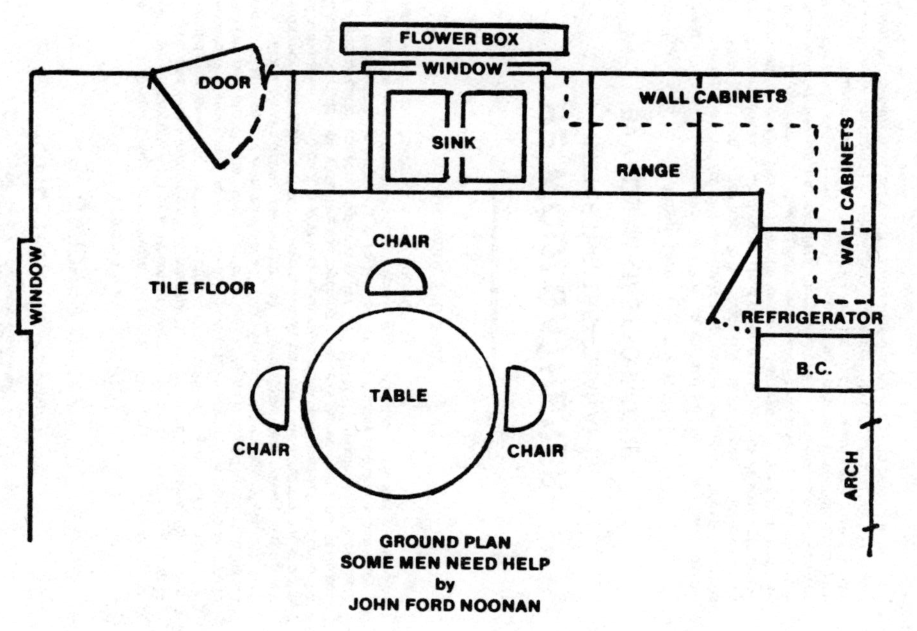

GROUND PLAN
SOME MEN NEED HELP
by
JOHN FORD NOONAN

Other Publications for Your Interest

SEA MARKS

(LITTLE THEATRE—DRAMA)

By GARDNER McKAY

1 woman, 1 man—Unit set

Winner of L.A. Drama Critics Circle Award "Best Play." This is the "funny, touching, bittersweet tale" (Sharbutt, A.P.) of a fisherman living on a remote island to the west of Ireland who has fallen in love with, in retrospect, a woman he's glimpsed only once. Unschooled in letter-writing, he tries his utmost to court by mail and, after a year-and-a-half, succeeds in arranging a rendezvous at which, to his surprise, she persuades him to live with her in Liverpool. Their love affair ends only when he is forced to return to the life he better understands. "A masterpiece." (The Tribune, Worcester, Mass.) "Utterly winning," (John Simon, New York Magazine.) "There's abundant humor, surprisingly honest humor, that grows between two impossible partners. The reaching out and the fearful withdrawal of two people who love each other but whose lives simply cannot be fused: a stubborn, decent, attractive and touching collision of temperments, honest in portraiture and direct in speech. High marks for SEA MARKS!" (Walter Kerr, New York Times.) "Fresh as a May morning. A lovely, tender and happily humorous love story." (Elliot Norton, Boston Herald American.) "It could easily last forever in actors' classrooms and audition studios." (Oliver, The New Yorker)

(Royalty, $50-$40)

THE WOOLGATHERER

(LITTLE THEATRE—DRAMA)

By WILLIAM MASTROSIMONE

1 man, 1 woman—Interior

In a dreary Philadelphia apartment lives Rose, a shy and slightly creepy five-and-dime salesgirl. Into her life saunters Cliff, a hard-working, hard-drinking truck driver—who has picked up Rose and been invited back to her room. Rose is an innocent whose whole life centers around reveries and daydreams. He is rough and witty—but it's soon apparent—just as starved for love as she is. This little gem of a play was a recent success at New York's famed Circle Repertory starring Peter Weller and Patricia Wettig. Actors take note: *The Woolgatherer* has several excellent monologues. ". . . energy, compassion and theatrical sense are there."—N.Y. Times. ". . . another emotionally wrenching experience no theatre enthusiast should miss."—Rex Reed. "Mastrosimone writes consistently witty and sometimes lyrical dialogue."—New York Magazine. "(Mastrosimone) has a knack for composing wildly humorous lines at the same time that he is able to penetrate people's hearts and dreams."—Hollywood Reporter.

(Royalty, $50-$40)

Other Publications for Your Interest

TALKING WITH . . .

(LITTLE THEATRE)

By JANE MARTIN

11 women—Bare stage

Here, at last, is the collection of eleven extraordinary monologues for eleven actresses which had them on their feet cheering at the famed Actors Theatre of Louisville—audiences, critics and, yes, even jaded theatre professionals. The mysteriously pseudonymous Jane Martin is truly a "find", a new writer with a wonderfully idiosyncratic style, whose characters alternately amuse, move and frighten us always, however, speaking to use from the depths of their souls. The characters include a baton twirler who has found God through twirling; a fundamentalist snake handler, an ex-rodeo rider crowded out of the life she has cherished by men in 3-piece suits who want her to dress up "like Minnie damn Mouse in a tutu"; an actress willing to go to any length to get a job; and an old woman who claims she once saw a man with "cerebral walrus" walk into a McDonald's and be healed by a Big Mac. "Eleven female monologues, of which half a dozen verge on brilliance."—London Guardian. "Whoever (Jane Martin) is, she's a writer with an original imagination."—Village Voice. "With Jane Martin, the monologue has taken on a new poetic form, intensive in its method and revelatory in its impact."—Philadelphia Inquirer. "A dramatist with an original voice . . . (these are) tales about enthusiasms that become obsessions, eccentric confessionals that levitate with religious symbolism and gladsome humor."—N.Y. Times. *Talking With . . .* is the 1982 winner of the American Theatre Critics Association Award for Best Regional Play. (#22009)

(Royalty, $60-$40.
If individual monologues are done separately: Royalty, $15-$10.)

HAROLD AND MAUDE

(ADVANCED GROUPS—COMEDY)

By COLIN HIGGINS

9 men, 8 women—Various settings

Yes: *the Harold and Maude!* This is a stage adaptation of the wonderful movie about the suicidal 19 year-old boy who finally learns how to truly *live* when he meets up with that delightfully whacky octogenarian, Maude. Harold is the proverbial Poor Little Rich Kid. His alienation has caused him to attempt suicide several times, though these attempts are more cries for attention than actual attempts. His peculiar attachment to Maude, whom he meets at a funeral (a mutual passion), is what saves him—and what captivates us. This new stage version, a hit in France directed by the internationally-renowned Jean-Louis Barrault, will certainly delight both afficionados of the film and new-comers to the story. "Offbeat upbeat comedy."—Christian Science Monitor. (#10032)

(Royalty, $60-$40.)

THE SEA HORSE

EDWARD J. MOORE

(Little Theatre) Drama

I Man, I Woman, Interior

It is a play that is, by turns, tender, ribald, funny and suspenseful. Audiences everywhere will take it to their hearts because it is touched with humanity and illuminates with glowing sympathy the complexities of a man-woman relationship. Set in a West Coast waterfront bar, the play is about Harry Bales, a seaman, who, when on shore leave, usually heads for "The Sea Horse," the bar run by Gertrude Blum, the heavy, unsentimental proprietor. Their relationship is purely physical and, as the play begins, they have never confided their private yearnings to each other. But this time Harry has returned with a dream: to buy a charter fishing boat and to have a son by Gertrude. She, in her turn, has made her life one of hard work, by day, and nocturnal love-making; she has encased her heart behind a facade of toughness, utterly devoid of sentimentality, because of a failed marriage. Irwin's play consists in the ritual of "dance" courtship by Harry of Gertrude, as these two outwardly abrasive characters fight, make up, fight again, spin dreams, deflate them, make love and reveal their long locked-up secrets.

"A burst of brilliance!"—*N.Y. Post.* "I was touched close to tears!"—*Village Voice.* "A must! An incredible love story. A beautiful play!"—*Newhouse Newspapers.* "A major new playwright!"—*Variety.*

ROYALTY, $50–$35

THE AU PAIR MAN

HUGH LEONARD

(Little Theatre) Comedy

I Man, I Woman, Interior

The play concerns a rough Irish bill collector named Hartigan, who becomes a love slave and companion to an English lady named Elizabeth, who lives in a cluttered London town house, which looks more like a museum for a British Empire on which the sun has long set. Even the door bell chimes out the national anthem. Hartigan is immediately conscripted into her service in return for which she agrees to teach him how to be a gentleman rather after the fashion of a reverse Pygmalion. The play is a wild one, and is really the never-ending battle between England and Ireland. Produced to critical acclaim at Lincoln Center's Vivian Beaumont Theatre.

ROYALTY, $50–$35

Other Publications for Your Interest

A WEEKEND NEAR MADISON

(LITTLE THEATRE—COMIC DRAMA)

By KATHLEEN TOLAN

2 men, 3 women—Interior

This recent hit from the famed Actors Theatre of Louisville, a terrific ensemble play about male-female relationships in the 80's, was praised by *Newsweek* as "warm, vital, glowing . . . full of wise ironies and unsentimental hopes". The story concerns a weekend reunion of old college friends now in their early thirties. The occasion is the visit of Vanessa, the queen bee of the group, who is now the leader of a lesbian/feminist rock band. Vanessa arrives at the home of an old friend who is now a psychiatrist hand in hand with her naif-like lover, who also plays in the band. Also on hand are the psychiatrist's wife, a novelist suffering from writer's block; and his brother, who was once Vanessa's lover and who still loves her. In the course of the weekend, Vanessa reveals that she and her lover desperately want to have a child—and she tries to persuade her former male lover to father it, not understanding that he might have some feelings about the whole thing. *Time Magazine* heard "the unmistakable cry of an infant hit . . . Playwright Tolan's work radiates promise and achievement." (#25051)

(Royalty, $60-$40.)

PASTORALE

(LITTLE THEATRE—COMEDY)

By DEBORAH EISENBERG

3 men, 4 women—Interior
(plus 1 or 2 bit parts and 3 optional extras)

"Deborah Eisenberg is one of the freshest and funniest voices in some seasons."—Newsweek. Somewhere out in the country Melanie has rented a house and in the living room she, her friend Rachel who came for a weekend but forgets to leave, and their school friend Steve (all in their mid-20s) spend nearly a year meandering through a mental landscape including such concerns as phobias, friendship, work, sex, slovenliness and epistemology. Other people happen by: Steve's young girlfriend Celia, the virtuous and annoying Edie, a man who Melanie has picked up in a bar, and a couple who appear during an intense conversation and observe the sofa is on fire. The lives of the three friends inevitably proceed and eventually draw them, the better prepared perhaps by their months on the sofa, in separate directions. "The most original, funniest new comic voice to be heard in New York theater since Beth Henley's 'Crimes of the Heart.'"—N.Y. Times. "A very funny, stylish comedy."—The New Yorker. "Wacky charm and wayward wit."—New York Magazine. "Delightful."—N.Y. Post. "Uproarious . . . the play is a world unto itself, and it spins."—N.Y. Sunday Times. (#18016)

(Royalty, $50-$35.)